MY LIFE SO FAR

(A collection of poetry)

MOET WILLIAMS

Moet Williams

MY LIFE SO FAR

Table of contents

Introduction

Thank you for taking the time to peruse my literary work. My passion for writing dates back to my adolescence, and since then, I have been a vocal proponent of the art form. My writing has since matured, and I am eager to share my progress with you through this book.

Despite the challenges that I have encountered in my life, writing has been a constant source of solace. At times, I questioned my abilities and feared that I had lost my passion, but I eventually realized that this was far from the truth. Through my poetry, I have been able to convey my life story, and I hope that you will take the time to read and appreciate my work.

I understand that some individuals may critique my poetry, but I am grateful for the opportunity to share my talent with the world. It took me a considerable amount of time to muster the courage to produce this book, but I hope that my work will enable you to gain a better understanding of me.

Thank you for taking the time to read my poetry.

Can you believe it?

Can you believe it?
that at 13 I was depressed
Can you believe it?
that I'm afraid of my past coming back to haunt me
Can you believe it?
that at 14 I was happy
Can you believe it?
that my happiness didn't last long
Can you believe it?
that I turned to pain as a way out
Can you believe it?
that I turned to music as a way out also
Can you believe it?
that at 15 I fell in love
Can you believe it?
that my first love hurt me deeply
can you believe
that for a brief second I was happy
Can you believe it?
that I was still turning to pain and music as a way out
Can you believe it?
that i'm still 15 and I'm still afraid of my past
Can you believe it?
that I'm now afraid for my future

Life and love

I once met a girl
who at 15 fell in Love
with a guy who was 19
they dated for a month
and it was the worst month of her life
she realized that she was in love but he wasn't
when they broke up
she was heart broken
she kept it all inside
she had other boyfriends
but she didn't want them
she wanted him
by the time she was single
he found someone new and fell in love
again heartbroken
she begin to go to pain and music
to deal with the heartbreak
of losing the one she loves

Knowing the unknown

What is love?
Love is laughing so hard you can't Breath
Love is smiling till it hurts
Love is crying till you can't cry no More
What is life?
Life is tears
Life is smiles
Life is mistakes and lessons
What is me and you?
I don't know what you and me is
Is it love? is it forever?
Is it never? I don't know
Do you know what me and you are?
Do you know if it is love? if it is Forever?
If it is never? do you know?
In life there is a sense of the Unknowing
You never know what life holds for us
So you chose your path in life
Love is unknowing
You could mistake love for lust
Love won't last forever
In both love and life
There is a sense of the unknowing
Can you figure it out

Invisible girl

Invisible girl
That's me
No one can see me
Invisible
Is me
Invisible girl
That's me
No one can hear me
Invisible
Is me
Invisible girl
That's me
The ghost of darkness
Invisible
Is me
Invisible girl
That's me
Proud of it
Invisible
Is me
Invisible girl
That's me
Embracing it
Invisible
Is me

I am

I am
pretty
smart
funny
I am
an actor
a singer
a poet
I am
a writer
a painter
a song writer
I am
different

Human

undefined
Human
This one word
has a lot to say
can it be defined
Human
It defines anybody
who can define it
everybody can
Human
can be a person
dead or alive
so can it be defined
Human
it can be defined
it defines me
I am H.U.M.A.N

Dead dreams

I have high hopes for my life
I want to be an actor some day
I have the skills to do a lot of things
I have low hopes for my life
I do not think I can be a poet or actor some day
I do not think I have the skills for that
I have no hope for my life
I think I am still the indivisible girl
I have no hope in my life
I have no dreams
My dreams are dead

Blinded by the past

Blinded by the fear.
Blinded by the past
Chained away from the future
Blinded by the pain of the past
Blinded by the hate of the past
Chained by the fear
You can see the future
It's in your hands, but the past holds you back
Why? Cause you can't let go of the past.
Let the past go
Let the love in
Stop being blind and love him
He's worth it. He's earned the key to your heart.

Love is

Love is
A 4 letter word
that has no meaning
Love is
A 4 letter word
nobody knows the true meaning of
Love is
a 4 letter word
that lost meaning in the world
Love is
A 4 letter word
that people use to destroy hearts
Love is
a 4 letter word
and nothing more but a 4 letter word
My first
You are my first friend
you are my first crush
you are my first boyfriend
you are my first love
you are my first broken heart
you are my first physical scar
you are my first emotional scar
you are my first
you are my last

Second Chance

Cutting her wrists
deeper and deeper
she is about ready to leave
leave this earth and never come back
she looks up and she can see god
He says it is not your time
it is not your time to be with me
Her mother beating on her bedroom door
Her mom kicks the door down
she sees her baby passed out on the floor bleeding
she calls 911
She wakes up in a hospital bed
She got a second chance
A second chance at life

Harsh Reality

Nigga claim he loves me
Cares for me
Only want me
Left so many times
Then came right back
Talking about he'll never leave again.
But turns around and threats to leave
How do I live like this?
Wanna leave? But I know I'll be right back
A vicious cycle I'm stuck in
How do I get out of it?
Don't know what to do.
Tired of this life
Trying to figure out what to do
Know I love him
Know I can't live without
How do I live?
I can't believe a word he says
I can't trust his word
Tired of the cycle I'm in
Just wanna scream out
Just wanna break out of it
Don't know how?
Don't know what to do anymore.
You was the same nigga I stayed up for
Same nigga I put up with
All the accusations from you

All the fights
All the name calling
I stayed and you go and break my heart
Did what you accused me of doing
And what makes it worse with an ex of yours.
Got me analyzing my body
Figuring out the pain I'm feeling
Hating myself
Feeling so ugly wishing for the dream to be over
Sadly it's not a dream, it's a harsh reality.

Nobody knows

Nobody knows
the pain I go through to coop
Nobody knows
How much blood I see every time
Nobody knows
why I go through it
Nobody knows
the pain of my past
Nobody knows
Why I'm afraid of my past
Nobody knows
why my future is just as scary as my past
Nobody knows
And I'm not ready to tell why

Loving an old flame

Loving and old flame all over again....
The irony in that
My ex bf is my baby...
I'll always love him
My old love refurbished
Into a deeper love
Into a deeper connection.
Into something stronger and solid
Loving him all over again
Loving my best friend all over again....
I fall deeper in love everyday
All over again
He does no wrong
I have not hate for anything he does
I love everything about him
I'm happy again with him
Yay

The voices

Voices in my head screaming
Voices screaming for help
As death comes near the voices get louder
Bright lights shining, more voices
But maybe it's all In my head
No one knows I'm dying
No one knows I am here in this position
No one cares enough to see
Voices in my head screaming out
Voices screaming for help
As death grows near
The voices in my head grow silent.
Life flashing before my eyes
Wishing that dying was faster
Painless, but slow death
An inner war
Everyday there is a war inside me
My heart and my mind fighting
My heart screams out louder
Than my mind, but there's still war
My heart and mind fight everyday
My mind can say one thing
My heart another
Screaming at the top of their lungs at each other
And then silence is left
As one battle has ended, but the war hasn't

It's an everyday battle
Between my heart and mind
Everytime the battle ends I'm left to decide who's right?
My heart or my mind
Who I should listen to?
My heart or my mind.
I somehow mistakenly choose my mind
My mind I always seems to listen to
My heart always seems to silence or cage it, but never free it.
I have a heart caged away.
I have a heart screaming to be listened to
A heart wanting to be free.
There's a war inside me everyday
A war I can only stop by freeing my heart from its cage

Love, scary?

Love, scary?
Maybe
There's always something to be afraid
Love is one
Love, hurtful?
No, it may seem like it but no
It's peaceful to love in caged
It's beautiful.
Love, scary?
Yeah, but it's worth it.
Loving someone unconditional and uncaged is worth it

Questions

Question after question swirl in my mind everyday

Question after question form in my head that I am and was to scared to ask you and them

Hate fueling up in my body everyday since the day

Hate pouring out of me at people that dont deserve it

For so long I have been afraid of the dark

For so long I have been afraid of you... of myself and how far this razor can go

For so long I have been guilty of it all.

Question after question make shape in my mind everyday

Question after question runs through my mind like a track star everyday

Depression is getting stronger and stronger as time goes by

Life goes on and time goes on without a care in the world for us humans and our emotions

To afraid to speak to you or anyone about the incident

To afraid everyday to sleep in the dark every night

My fear and hatred and anger and depression takes over and overwhelms me like boulders daily

Question after question pushed deeper and deeper into the back of my mind

Question after question cloud my mind like a thick fog

Long nights and rough mornings get harder and harder to deal with

All the booze and drugs in the world don't help clear the fog

On a daily basis I look for some type of numbing to just be okay for one night

Just in search of one night of bliss and peace..... Just one night

Long Distance Love Story

I was hurting when you came along
I didn't know how it should feel to be loved
I tried to be perfect, but no one is perfect
We ain't perfect, but the love we share is perfect
Our date, I'll never forget
Even if I do you will be the to help me remember
I get a heart push when your name comes across my phone
Still got a crush on you even though you are mine
A queen on my throne, next to you my king
Wishing everyday to touch your face
The distance is killing me
Our love with each FaceTime call
Asking the man upstairs for a different type of love
Took me months to see I had what I was praying for
Been through hell and back for someone who didn't want me for years
I know if we go through hell, we will reach heaven
So far away from each other
I need you here
I need to know your feelings
Sucky ass distance, stronger love
I miss sleeping on the phone with you at night
Your voice, my Lullaby
I can't imagine life without you
All I want is you
I don't know what I'll do without you my love

Probably lose my mind
We a secret nonetheless
Society would judge us
Society would try to destroy us
One day we will see each other
The distance won't be so bad soon enough
Miles apart yet stronger together
Sucky ass distance, stronger love

Acknowledgements

As I reminisce about my life's journey, I am filled with immense gratitude towards the individuals who have played a pivotal role in shaping me into the person I am today. These people have been my guiding light and have helped me navigate through the ups and downs of life. I want to express my heartfelt appreciation to those who have inspired me to write every piece that you have just read. They have been a source of inspiration and have fueled my creativity. My family and friends hold a special place in my heart, as their unwavering support and constant encouragement have been a driving force behind my passion. This book is a culmination of my life's work, representing my experiences, struggles and triumphs. I never imagined that I would be able to see it through at my age, but with the help of those around me, I was able to bring it to fruition. For those who have read my book, I am deeply grateful for your time and attention. It is my hope that it has given you a glimpse into my life and experiences, allowing you to connect with me on a deeper level. Seeing my dream come to fruition has been an incredibly humbling and fulfilling experience, and I owe it all to the unwavering support of those around me. From the bottom of my heart, I thank you for being a part of my journey.

www.ingramcontent.com/pod-product-compliance
Ingram Content Group UK Ltd.
Pitfield, Milton Keynes, MK11 3LW, UK
UKHW021654190726
13853UKWH00001B/256

9 798869 218704